SEARCHING FOR *sea glass*

JOURNEYING WITH GOD THROUGH CHRONIC ILLNESS

– 30 DEVOTIONALS –

Kara J. Plett

Lynn + Everett,
Praying God
meets you in a
special way as
you continue this
journey.
-Kara

First Printing 2021

Facebook: Kara J Plett Author

Front Cover Image: Adobe Stock www.adobestock.com

Book Design: Anne Kuykendall www.pagedynamics.ca

Table of Contents

We don't have to journey alone.

He is right beside us

every step of the way.

Searching for Sea Glass

"Here, you can have this back. It's garbage!" My four-year-old niece had just dropped a handful of sea glass in my outstretched hand. I had given her some "treasures from the beach" – a variety of shells and sea glass. The shells were what she wanted to keep and saw as pretty but to her, the pieces of sea glass were just garbage.

I wondered how I could explain to her why the pieces of glass are so beautiful to me. How I take every chance I get in my travels to go to the beach to search for bits of green, brown, clear or even the rare piece of blue glass. I think to myself, when she's older, I will tell her about sea glass.

For now, I will remember how God speaks to me as I search for bits of colour on the beach. Each piece I find is a reminder that He is refining me. The once-broken pieces of glass – "garbage" – have been turned into treasures through the constant buffeting of the waves, scraping on the sand, crashing into rocks and eventually ending up on a beach where someone with a watchful eye may spot their beauty.

We are all rough and broken but God uses events, people, and circumstances in our lives to wear away the sharp edges; to soften and shape us into who He knows we can be.

The following pages are devotions from my search for "sea glass" in my chronic illnesses. Maybe you are holding this book because you too have an illness. I know this can be a lonely path but I truly believe that as Christ followers we don't have to journey alone. He is right beside us every step of the way and He can use our illnesses to make us more beautiful if we draw close to Him in the process and strive to catch His perspective.

These devotions are written with the hope that you will actively participate in them. I pray that each devotion you read, and each exercise you do, will point you to HIM. When you sit with God and His Word, with a pen in hand, He often meets you in special ways. Please complete the devotions as you feel led – you set the pace. I have experienced God in so many new ways during these last few years of illness. I find myself returning to these devotions in the midst of the struggles that emerge again and again in my life. God is faithful each time I press into Him to grant me His precious peace.

May my search for "sea glass" – the beauty in the refinement of a chronic illness – allow you to see hope and transformation in the struggles and challenges of your life as well.

To Him who is able to do so much more than we can ever ask or imagine,

Kara

How High

I don't know the story of the diagnosis of your chronic illness. I do know everyone has a different journey. For me, there were several years of not knowing what was going on – not being able to dress myself, my husband having to help me get on my way to work in the morning, then hobbling into the school and trying to be the best teacher I could be, despite how I was feeling. It took time for the doctors to determine what was wrong.

One of the things I found difficult during this time, and even after the diagnosis of rheumatoid arthritis and later fibromyalgia, was living it out in front of people. When you have an invisible illness it's hard for people to understand what you're going through – it even takes time to understand it yourself.

I began to ask God to help me. I knew I couldn't keep worrying about how others saw me. There is a scripture that brought me such comfort then, and it still does today.

For this reason I kneel before the Father, from whom every family in heaven and on earth derives its name. I pray that out of his glorious riches he may strengthen you with power through his Spirit in your inner being, so that Christ may dwell in your hearts through faith. And I pray that you, being rooted and established in love, may have power, together with all the Lord's holy people, to grasp how wide and long and high and deep is the love of Christ, and to know this love that surpasses knowledge – that you may be filled to the measure of all the fullness of God.

Ephesians 3:14-21

Reading these verses fills me with His love but pausing to meditate on them fills me with a more complete and deeper understanding.

He wants to strengthen me. Christ wants to dwell in my heart. He wants me to recognize how wide, long, high and deep the love of Christ is. It surpasses all knowledge. I can be filled beyond measure with God's love.

When I read this I realize that God loves me beyond my knowledge. I can't begin to understand the size of it. If He loves me this much, I can share my sorrow, confusion, pain, and frustration with Him. I don't need to look to others for acceptance and understanding. I can find it in Him. I am not alone! I want to grab hold of this truth!

Being fully loved by God allows me to accept what others can offer with thanks – not wishing for something different from them. I have all that I need already – the rest is a gift.

Why not try writing out Ephesians 3:14-21 today – the simple act of writing out a scripture in your own hand will help you process the words more deeply in your heart and mind. As you write, meditate on the words and allow God to minister to your heart.

O, how He loves you.

Perfect Peace

I couldn't sleep last night. I was lying there wide awake thinking about the future. What does this illness mean for my job for our finances? Fear began to overtake me. God began to remind me of a way to help me replace the fear and worry with His Word.

Years ago, I had searched for a scripture to help quiet my mind and found God pointing me to Isaiah 26:3, "You will keep him in perfect peace, Whose mind is stayed on You." (NKJV) I memorized this scripture and have often repeated it to myself in times of worry. It's my go-to scripture.

Beyond repeating this scripture I have found it powerful to look at each of the words in the verse one by one. To let the truth of each word ring out in my mind. I've also found it helpful to write it out so that it becomes even more a part of my heart and I can recall it easily in times like this.

It might look something like this as I meditate on what each word means, one at a time:

You (God, ruler of ALL)

You will (He says He WILL, not He might)

You will keep (He will always be there)

You will keep him (or her – that's me!)

You will keep him in perfect (the best, no flaws)

You will keep him in perfect peace (a place of no worries – beyond my understanding)

You will keep him in perfect peace, Whose mind (my thoughts, how I choose to think)

You will keep him in perfect peace, Whose mind is stayed (steadfast, stay put)

You will keep him in perfect peace, Whose mind is stayed on You (my Saviour, the One who knows all my tomorrows and cares for me!)

You will keep him in perfect peace, Whose mind is stayed on You!

I did this again today as the fear and worry felt overwhelming and His perfect peace filled my mind and heart.

Can I encourage you to try this with Isaiah 26:3? Or maybe you have a favourite scripture of your own. Use this page to write the scripture out word by word emphasizing each as in the example on the previous page. As you write, pray that God will use His Word actively in your mind and heart and press away the fear and worry.

Father, thank you for planting Your Word in our hearts and minds.

Masterpiece

Much to my consternation, my husband insists on having a framed picture of me on his bedside table. These days I find myself responding negatively when I catch a glimpse of myself in that frame. Even though my husband says he loves what he sees, I avoid looking at myself. When I look at the recent photo, all I see is fatigue, pain, and someone who is just trying to carry on. I see my diagnosis and all the things I'm not able to do anymore.

As the Spirit prompts me to battle this today, He brings to mind an activity that I have asked the ladies in my Bible Study to do in previous years. I grab that framed picture of myself and make a quick black and white photocopy of it, pick up my Bible and get to work.

I turn to Psalm 139:1-18. As I read, I'm reminded how well God knows me. I jot down some of the ideas from the verses around my photo. Things like: You surround me – even in the dark places. You know every one of my thoughts. Thank you for hemming me in behind and before – I need this right now. You made me intricately and wonderfully – even if it doesn't always feel like it. You made me exactly the way I am for a purpose – help me to know what that is now. I need your hand on me. You are a safe place. You know ALL my days – including these days with my illness. You remind me that I am so beautiful to You.

I let God speak to me through His Word and talk to Him about the changes in myself the past while. I let Him assure me that He still has a plan for me as His wonderful creation. It's hard to keep looking at the picture of myself but as I do, and as I keep journaling around my picture, I start to see myself as God sees me.

Finally, and most importantly, I feel a nudge from the Spirit to sign the artist's name in the bottom corner of the picture. The artist is God! I let His name speak mightily to me of how He is pleased with me – HIS MASTERPIECE. See Ephesians 2:10 (NLT).

My illness doesn't change this. What I can't do anymore doesn't change this. How I look doesn't change this.

Your illness doesn't change who you are to God either.

May I encourage you to try this activity and let God speak of how He sees you? Glue a picture of yourself on the facing page and spend time in Psalm 139 journaling around your picture. Don't forget to put the Artist's signature on it – He's so proud to call you His.

I'm thankful that we are marvelously made, just the way we are right now! May we live in the confidence of this every day.

You are His *masterpiece.*

Anxious

"Do not be anxious about anything."

But I am.

I'm anxious about what people think of me, I'm anxious about my appointment with my doctor. I'm anxious about the future. Then I start to become anxious because I'm not supposed to feel anxious.

Can you relate?

Today I sat with my Bible and filled my journal with all kinds of anxious thoughts. I was feeling frustrated with myself. Trying in vain to combat the thoughts and feelings racing inside my head. I asked God for wisdom and felt Him leading me to the following scripture. It came alive in a new way for me today. I hope it will for you too.

Do not be anxious about anything, but in everything by prayer and supplication with thanksgiving let your requests be made known to God. And the peace of God, which surpasses all understanding, will guard your hearts and minds in Christ Jesus.

Philippians 4:6-7 (ESV)

Have you ever paraphrased a scripture as if God were speaking to you? That's what I felt prompted to do with this verse. The words in brackets are things I felt God reminding me of:

Kara, do not be anxious about anything (*what others think of you, the appointments, the paperwork you have to fill out*), but in everything (*that includes your illness and how it impacts your life*), by prayer (*TALK to ME*) and supplication (*ask earnestly and humbly – get down on your knees if it helps*), with thanksgiving (*knowing that gratitude will change your mindset – STOP NOW – write down what you're thankful for: your husband, your parents...*), let your requests be made known to God (*to Me*). And the peace of God which surpasses ALL understanding (*you know, that inexpressible calm*), will guard your hearts and minds (*let the other thoughts and feelings fade away, take them captive*) IN Christ Jesus (*who died for you so you can join Me in eternity*).

Wow! Once God and I had this conversation that PEACE that passes our understanding did come! I know the anxious thoughts may return, but He offers HIS peace again and again.

You can use this page to work through this same exercise using Philippians 4:6-7. Write out and paraphrase this scripture yourself. Talk to God about what He wants you to notice as you spend time with Him. Remember, God's Word is alive and active and ready to change us.

Who I Am

I introduced myself to someone today and it was such a strange experience. Let me explain why.

"Hi I'm Kara, I'm a..."

Normally, I would fill in the blank with "teacher." If I'm honest, I really liked being able to introduce myself this way because of how my occupation defined me. But right now I'm on leave. I'm not able to 'be' a teacher. So much of who I am is wrapped up in that description..."I'm a teacher."

When something comes along and disrupts how we see ourselves it's hard. Have you wrestled with this? Has your illness caused you to feel like you're on unstable footing with your identity?

I am having to reexamine my identity right now and this is a good thing because my identity isn't, "I'm a teacher." It's so much more than that. My identity is in Christ and who He says I am! And so I find myself thinking about this today. Needing a reset when it comes to identity.

Here is a list of verses about who God says we are. There's a short description beside each verse but don't miss out on reading the entire scripture in a translation you love. God's Word is powerful and will speak truth into our lives. As you read through these scriptures (even aloud) I encourage you to use the facing page to write down what God says about you. Scatter these thoughts all over the page. Write some of them boldly or in all capitals to emphasize what God wants you to hear.

Child of God John 1:12; 1 John 3:1
Friend John 15:15
Loved Colossians 3:12
Wonderfully Made Psalm 139:14
Beloved Jeremiah 31:3
Masterpiece Ephesians 2:10; Psalm 139:14
Co-heir Romans 8:17
Forgiven Psalm 86:5; 1 John 1:9
Chosen 1 Peter 2:9; Ephesians 1:4
New Creation 2 Corinthians 5:17
More than a Conquerer Romans 8:37
Work in Progress Philippians 1:6
Provided for Philippians 4:19
Victorious 1 Corinthians 15:57
Ambassadors 2 Corinthians 5:20
A Branch John 15:5
Sons/Daughters Galatians 3:26; Ephesians 1:5
Heirs Romans 8:17
Citizens of Heaven Philippians 3:20
Justified Romans 5:1
Light Matthew 5:14; 1Thesalonnians 5:5
New Ephesians 4:24
Salt Matthew 5:13

Did you catch who God says you are? I sure did and thank Him for the value He gives me in my identity in Him. Other parts of my identity may change but who I am in Christ remains unchanged in Him.

O Father, help us rest in this.

Groaning

I 'hit a wall' yesterday and fell down in a slump beside it. I couldn't make myself do anything. I couldn't even express how I was feeling. I was just so tired of making myself carry on when everything felt so challenging with this body. So I lay at the bottom of the wall and Jesus met me there. No words, no scriptures, no motivational speeches, He just sat with me and heard my groaning.

In the same way, the Spirit helps us in our weaknesses. We do not know what we ought to pray for, but the Spirit himself intercedes for us through wordless groans. Romans 8:26

As Christians, we've been given the gift of the Holy Spirit. He is actually praying for us. We can rest at the feet of Jesus with only a groan escaping our lips and the Spirit is right there interceding on our behalf, telling God everything. He did this for me yesterday.

We may not know whether to pray for healing or to pray for strength to endure, but we can be assured the Spirit will always pray in accordance with the Word.

It also says the Spirit helps us in our weaknesses. I hate to be weak. To be the one who needs help. But this is exactly the time that the Spirit can enter in on my behalf – when I'm weak and willing to accept help. To intercede means to mediate, step in, plead, petition, entreat… Wow, having this done on my behalf is humbling and tells me how much I mean to God!

I'm so thankful that God's work in me is not limited by what I can express. The Spirit is praying for me!

Can you rest in this with me today? Maybe it's been a while since you've hit a wall and reached the point of groaning but we can probably all think of times when we have. What an encouragement to know that we can ask the Spirit to intercede for us right then and there and just sit at the feet of the One who knows us so well and loves us beyond what we can imagine.

On the facing page, read Romans 8:26 aloud as a prayer. Give thanks for a specific time when He has interceded on your behalf.

Father, thank you for meeting us right where we are!

Meanwhile, the moment we get tired in the waiting, God's Spirit is right alongside helping us along. If we don't know how or what to pray, it doesn't matter. He does our praying in and for us, making prayer out of our wordless sighs, our aching groans. He knows us far better than we know ourselves, knows our pregnant condition, and keeps us present before God. That's why we can be so sure that every detail in our lives of love for God is worked into something good.

Romans 8:26-28 (MSG)

Take Captive

I recently heard that most of us have more than 6,000 thoughts a day and that up to 80% of these are negative and 95% are repetitive. I don't know if these numbers are completely accurate but they give me pause. I know I tend to repeat negative thoughts to myself.

God has something to say about this in His Word. 2 Corinthians 10:5 tells us we need to take every thought captive to obey Christ. But how are we to do this? We may know that our minds are filling with pessimistic, negative, unhelpful thoughts but can we just tell ourselves to stop thinking this way? I've tried – it doesn't work for me.

If we look further, God has given us the solution. Philippians 4:8 says,

> "Finally, brothers and sisters, whatever is true, whatever is noble, whatever is right, whatever is pure, whatever is lovely, whatever is admirable – if anything is excellent or praiseworthy – think about such things."

When I fill my mind with what is true, noble, right, pure, lovely, admirable, excellent or praiseworthy, there isn't much space left for the negative thoughts.

Following is an exercise I've done to help me focus on my thinking. I hope you'll give it a try. This may sound strange but please use a pencil to start with.

What are your thoughts on challenging days? Maybe you're thinking things like, I don't have any purpose. No one understands. I'm so alone. I used to be so capable. As you identify a negative thought write it down with your pencil. Draw a thought bubble around it. Write down the negative, unhelpful, and pessimistic thoughts that come to mind.

Now, really focus on the list in Philippians 4:8. Read it over several times, even aloud. Then begin to review the negative thoughts on your page. Ask God to counter them with the way He has asked us to think. Erase each negative thought and replace it in pen with these new thoughts, taking each one captive. For example, erase "I'm so alone" and replace it with what is true, "God never leaves me."

Here's the thing. Our thoughts may not easily adjust to God's way of thinking. We need to discipline our thinking whenever the Spirit prompts us. If we get in the habit of acting on these promptings, intentionally replacing negative thoughts with the things God has asked us to dwell on, it will begin to change the way we think and will renew our minds.

Maybe we can turn those percentages around! I'd like to try – will you join me?

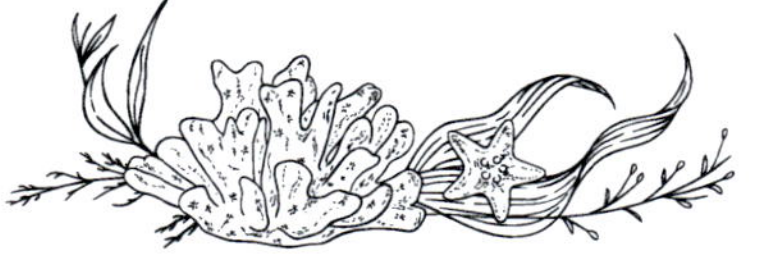

When I fill my mind with what is true, *noble, right, pure, lovely, admirable, excellent or praiseworthy, there isn't much space left for the negative thoughts.*

He Stood Still

It happened again today. I woke up not feeling well. I tried to carry on like everything was fine and before I knew it my mind began to mull over so many things that had been bothering me – and it snowballed from there. It started small with frustration about a new ministry opportunity. Questioning whether my body could take it on or if I said no how this would look to others. It grew bigger as I thought about physio exercises I've been putting so much effort into. They don't seem to be helping the pain. It rolled on as I looked at my husband and wished I had more to give him. Another layer was added as I lamented the desire to invite others over for a get together but didn't trust my body would feel well enough. Pretty soon that 'snowball' was so big and heavy that the tears came. Tears of sorrow and I'll admit self-pity.

I cried out to God – what do I do with this? These feelings are real and so overwhelming today. I just want to sit and cry. But I know Satan is using this – he loves it when I'm defeated.

Have you heard the story of blind Bartimaeus? (Mark 10:46-52) On the facing page you will see a song I wrote about it many years ago – God brought it to mind again today. Jesus was a busy man. As He was traveling with His disciples they passed by a man (Bartimaeus) begging by the side of the road. He was blind since birth – I think he had a heavy burden of sorrow too. When Bartimaeus heard that it was Jesus passing by he didn't just sit, he called out, "Jesus, Son of David, have mercy on me!" And Jesus heard him and stood still. He stood still, heard his cry and healed him.

Like Bartimaeus I need to call out for mercy. Here I sit amidst my pain, seemingly blind to the hope that I can have in Christ. He wants me to call out and when I do He stands still for me too. He hears me and heals me. How amazing that He takes the time to see me! To stand still for me!

He wants to do this for each of us. Do you have a 'snowball' of sorrow today? Jesus is walking by. Call out to Him. He will hear you and He will stand still ready to offer healing that only He can give. This may be a physical healing. Or maybe a peace that passes your understanding. It could be a renewed determination that with Him you can carry on. Or the amazing gift of sitting with the God of all who cares about your sorrow.

Thank you, Jesus, for standing still for each of us who cry out to You.

Jesus, son of David, have mercy on me!

Jesus Stood Still

By Kara Plett

There sat the man
By the roadside
Blind was he and begging so
He heard the men
As they approached
Heard Christ's name
And he called out

Jesus, Son of David
Have mercy on me
Jesus, Son of David
Have mercy on me

And Jesus stood still
Jesus stood still
Jesus stood still
Heard the man's cry
Faith healed his eyes
To follow was now his cry

Here we all sit
Amidst our pain
Blind to the hope
Begging for grace

We know he's here
We know of His love
All we must do
Is to cry out

Jesus, Son of David
Have mercy on me
Jesus, Son of David
Have mercy on me

And Jesus stands still
Jesus stands still
Jesus stands still
He hears our cries
Faith heals our lives
To follow is now our cry

Who God Is

Some old Sunday School songs came to mind today. Songs about how strong and mighty God is, songs about His peace, songs about how much Jesus loves me. As a child, I would sing these songs out confidently at the top of my lungs. My understanding of who God is began at such a young age. These songs taught me about God's character. I'm thankful I grew up knowing Him as loving, mighty and a friend. I'm also grateful my understanding of God didn't end there.

I think back on when I first really came to understand God as forgiving and when I was truly thankful for His grace. There were times when I learned lessons about His faithfulness, and how I could trust that He is the judge and I don't have to be. Lately, I've been learning about Him as my shepherd. Like never before, I have rested at His feet and trusted that He will care for me right where I am.

I don't want to know just a bit about God – I want to know Him fully. There is always more to learn about Him. The more we get to know, the more we can trust Him in every situation we encounter, especially in challenging seasons.

Below you will see a list of scriptures that teach us about God's character (this is in no way an exhaustive list). Spend some time looking at what they say about who God is. Use the facing page to journal about His character. Thank Him for the times you have seen evidence of His character in your journey. Who is He to you today? Thank Him for continuing to reveal and show you more of who He is. Thank Him for the difficult circumstances that have made you aware of Him in a new way. Allow the scriptures to prompt, grow and encourage you today.

Comforter Psalm 23:4; Matthew 5:4
Counsellor Psalm 16:7
Everlasting 1Timothy 1:17
Friend James 2:23
Guide John 16:13
Holy 1 Peter 1:15-16)
Love 1 John 4:7-8
Rescuer Psalm 18:16-17
Saviour Titus 3:4-5
Sovereign Deuteronomy 3:24
Compassion James 5:11
Defender Romans 8:35, 36
Father Hebrews 12:5-9
Good Psalm 25:8; Nahum 1:7
Helper Isaiah 41:13
Judge James 4:12
Patient 2 Peter 3:9
Rock Matthew 7:24-25
Shepherd Psalm 23
Worthy Psalm 18:3

Thank you, Father, for who You are!

I have rested at His feet and *trusted* that He will care for me right where I am.

Armour of God

"Swords up!" My husband tells me this is what they would shout out in Sunday School while holding up their Bibles (swords). The teacher would then call out a scripture and everyone would race to see who could find the verse first. I can picture the kids, sitting on the edge of their seats, pages flipping wildly. My husband must have won the race often because he can always find a passage in the Bible before me. A kid's game, but one filled with so much truth.

> Stand firm then, with the belt of truth buckled around your waist, with the breastplate of righteousness in place, and with your feet fitted with the readiness that comes from the gospel of peace. In addition to all this, take up the shield of faith, with which you can extinguish all the flaming arrows of the evil one. Take the helmet of salvation and the sword of the Spirit, which is the word of God. And pray in the Spirit on all occasions with all kinds of prayers and requests. With this in mind, be alert and always keep on praying for all the Lord's people.
>
> Ephesians 6:14-18

I was thinking about the sword of the Spirit and each of the other pieces of armour relative to my current life and because there is a battle going on. Satan wants to use my illness to draw me away from God. But God wants the opposite – He wants me to draw near to Him.

Without the belt of truth, I could believe that God gave me this illness. But truth tells me that we live in a fallen world where we will have trouble (John 16:33).

My heart needs the protection of the breastplate. I am prone to act on my emotions when I'm tired and frustrated.

My feet need to be fitted for peace – striving for peace in my own heart, in my home and in my relationships so I can spread peace to others.

O, how I need a shield of faith – so often I don't know the plan, the whys, or see the full picture of where life is going. But I choose faith as the shield to protect me from the enemy's attacks.

And like my husband, I want to pick up my sword – the powerful Word of God – I want the scriptures so rooted in me that I can recognize truth at all times.

I want to intentionally put on each piece of armour, ultimately clothing myself in Christ.

Below, I have written a prayer. You can pray it yourself as often as you want or write one of your own.

He's given us the armour – let's put it on! Swords up!

Father, thank you for giving me your armour. I want to first put on your belt of truth. To go through this day recognizing your truth alone. Your truth holds everything together. You didn't give me this disease but You are walking with me in it. Satan wants to lie to me but I need Your truth to combat him. I want my decisions to be based on Your truth. Jesus, You are the way, the truth and the life!

I want to put on the breastplate of righteousness. I need You to protect my heart. My emotions can take over, especially when I don't feel well. I want to remember that it is through You that I am made new and spotless. There is no righteousness apart from You.

The sandals are next – footwear promoting peace. I can't live in the distraction of conflict – I need peace in my own life to promote peace to others. Peace that only comes from You. May the words that come from my mouth be Your words.

The shield of faith. Sometimes all I can do is just believe. I don't get to see or know everything. You know the plan. Thank you that You are growing my faith through this illness. When Satan tries to discourage me or lie to me, help me hold up the shield against his arrows of deceit. When I feel weak, help me ask others to hold up their shield beside mine or even directly in front of me. You haven't asked me to do this alone.

The helmet of salvation protects my mind and thoughts, Father. Life here on earth, with this illness, is just for a little while. Nothing can separate me from eternity with You. Thank you for the hope of heaven where we get to live fully healed.

Finally the sword of the Spirit. May Your Word be so instilled in my life that I can fight off the evil one with Your truth. I want Your Word to have full authority in my life. Help me to be able to recall Your words so that I can be fully equipped. You've given me this weapon, help me to use it.

Father, YOU are truth, righteousness, and peace. Salvation comes from You and Your Word is truth! As I go out today, may I walk in full confidence wearing Your armour.

In Jesus' name, Amen.

Cast It

Humble yourselves, therefore, under God's mighty hand, that He may lift you up in due time. Cast all your anxiety on him because he cares for you.
1 Peter 5:6-7

I find it hard to recognize pride in my own life and so the first part of this verse has really struck me this week. So often I don't feel "my stuff" is important enough to bring to God or even those close to me. But these verses tell me I benefit the most from God's care when I humble myself and share my anxieties with Him.

In His wisdom, God knows the things I hold back from Him can be used by the enemy as a foothold of worry or bitterness. What I see as small can become a heavy weight in no time when I try to "go it" on my own. When I say, "It's no big deal, I won't worry God with this," the small can start to become big. And then other "little" things pile on top of it. If I had cast that initial care on God and allowed Him to carry it in the first place I wouldn't be under a heavier and heavier weight.

I might even be angry or frustrated when I cast my anxiety on Him. God can handle this. I sometimes picture it as writing each of my worries on a piece of paper, crumpling them up and throwing them into the hands of God. I see Him patiently smoothing out the paper, and reading each one. Care emanating from His eyes.

If I truly lay down my pride and decide I don't need to carry these "little burdens" alone He will pick them up just like He promised. All of my worries matter to Him and I don't have to fall asleep with them rolling around in my mind or wake up and start the day with them again. I can cast them back on Him and trust Him to pick them up every time.

This doesn't mean that the worries and cares are going to be solved the second I throw them, or that they will be solved the way I think they should be. What it does mean is that the God who sees the whole picture of my life – is carrying the burdens through my journey.

My load can be lighter,
my mind can be freer,
my heart can be softer,
my Spirit at peace,
as I continue my journey.

Will you join me in humbling yourself and throwing your cares and anxieties on the One who wants to carry them for us. You can use this page to cast your anxieties into God's mighty hand. You could draw a hand with each of the worries laying in it. Or draw squares of paper and fill each one with a worry. Whatever you do, cast them on our Saviour.

He cares so much for each of us!

Every Good Gift

"How was your day?"

"Fine."

"What did you do?"

"Not much."

Sound familiar? Most of us have had this conversation.

I wonder if my conversations with God sometimes feel this way too. My response to Him can be so halfhearted when there is really so much in the day for me to recount to Him and praise Him for. But it takes my being attentive to His goodness throughout the day, especially on days I don't feel like it. I know it's gratitude that will help shift my mind to see what God has given me. And ultimately gratitude brings healing to my soul.

Every good and perfect gift is from above, coming down from the Father of the heavenly lights.
James 1:17

When I read this scripture I may think I don't have any 'good and perfect gifts' in my life right now. But if I believe in God's Word and His character, challenging circumstances shape me and point me to God – ultimately becoming a good gift from Him.

Here is something I've found helpful. I take time to write down everything that happened in my day – ordinary things like turning on my computer, brushing my teeth, making breakfast, taking medications, talking with a friend, having a nap before getting together with someone... After writing all of this down I go back through the list and thank God for the good in each event. The gift of clean water to brush my teeth, food to make breakfast, friends to talk with. Every good thing comes from Him.

What about those events that don't seem so good? Like taking medication or needing a nap. Can I still thank Him for these? I think so. I am thankful I have medication – what a provision. I'm thankful for the restoration of sleep. I praise Him for these things too.

So then, just as you received Christ Jesus as Lord, continue to live your life in him, rooted and built up in him, strengthened in the faith as you were taught, and overflowing with thankfulness.
Colossians 2:6-7

I want my life to so overflow with thankfulness that it spills out of me.

Will you try it? Write down everything that happened in your day. Go back through your list and thank God – give Him an offering of praise for the good gifts that can all be traced back to Him. Let your thanks fill you up so much that it overflows. Watch how it brings healing to your soul.

"How was *my* day?"

"Let me tell you – I am so blessed!"

I hope you're feeling blessed too.

Plans

I'm a planner. I like to dream, organize, and make lists to put things in motion. The reality these days is that my body so often changes my plans. But I don't want to let go of them.

I'm reminded of a story I have read to my grade 3 class almost every year, *Where the Red Fern Grows.*[1] In the book, a young boy is trying to catch a raccoon using a primitive trap his grandpa tells him how to make. His grandpa explains how the boy should drill a hole in a log and put something shiny inside. If he waits a few days, a coon will be sitting on the log with his paw in the hole grabbing for the shiny object unable to pull his fisted paw out of the hole. The boy asks his grandpa why the coon wouldn't just drop the object, remove his paw, and run away? His grandpa explains that the coon wants the shiny object so badly that he will keep his paw balled in a fist around the object preventing him from escaping. He is trapped because he just won't let go of what he wants.

Sometimes I feel like the coon – holding onto my plans so firmly that I'm trapped. All I need to do is open my hands that are so tightly grasping what I want, offer the plans to God, and walk in His freedom. But I don't.

Do you ever feel this way? Maybe the following verse will speak to you as it does to me.

In their hearts humans plan their course,
but the Lord establishes their steps.
Proverbs 16:9

I may make my plans but I have to have an open hand with them. God may have a different plan and in His wisdom may reorder my steps.

When I am wrestling with one of these situations, I find it helpful to actually clench my hands and talk to God about the plan I'm holding so tightly. As I release my wrestlings to Him, whatever they may be, I slowly open my hands. I continue doing this, sometimes needing to release the same thing several times as I talk with Him. I find the physical act of opening my clenched hands leads me into His peace.

I encourage you to try this yourself and experience God's peace washing over you as you release your plans to Him.

1. Wilson Rawls, *Where the Red Fern Grows* (United States: Doubleday, 1961), 58-59.

I invite you to write out Proverbs 16:9, write a prayer about your plans, thank the Lord for His wisdom in establishing your steps, or draw an open hand. Why not come back to this page when you feel yourself clutching at a plan. Let's ask Him today to help open our hands so we can live in the fullness of hope and freedom in Him. He is establishing our steps.

All I need to do is *open my hands* *that are so tightly grasping what I want, offer the plans to God, and walk in His freedom.*

Tulip

The heavens declare the glory of God; the skies proclaim the work of His hands. Day after day they pour forth speech; night after night they reveal knowledge.

Psalm 19:1-2

God loves to use His creation to speak to us. When was the last time He revealed something to you as you gazed at the world around you? Maybe it was the bud on a tree that gave you **hope** (Psalm 52:8). The chirping bird that reminded you of God's **care** for even that tiny bird and how much more He cares for you (Matthew 6:26). A snowflake's intricacy – declaring God's unique design in each piece of creation – including you, just the way you are (Psalm 139:14). Water trickling in the stream as if His **peace** were washing over you (Isaiah 48:18). Or that sunset that seemed like it was just for you...

Today, I noticed a tulip outside my front door. Now, I love tulips as much as the next person, but this particular location in my garden isn't supposed to have tulips; it's nicely mulched. But each year this one rogue tulip stretches itself towards the spring sunshine. God nudged me as I looked at it again today.

This tulip continues to bloom each year despite its less-than-hospitable surroundings. It made me think about my life. My illness makes many days less than hospitable for thriving. The burden of not feeling well is heavy. BUT when I press into Him, just like my tulip presses toward the sun, He carries me through. Each day I reach toward Him, He grows my perseverance and character. He encouraged me with this today.

I hope you'll find a time today or this week to sit with God in His creation. Look up the scriptures above, write one of them out, or ask Him to meet you where you are. Listen, look, smell. Talk to Him. What does He want to remind you of today? Maybe you could draw a picture on the facing page – I'm going to draw a picture of the tulip in the middle of the mulch and do some journaling.

Father, thank you for speaking to us through Your amazing creation.

Bind Them

I've been blessed with such an amazing heritage of faith. My parents and grandparents have all loved the Lord. They have passed on God's Word through their lives to those of us who have come after.

I was talking to my mom this morning and she was sharing a passage of scripture that she is memorizing. It impresses me that she wants to memorize scriptures and I love her reason for doing it – she wants to have God's Word planted firmly in her heart and mind.

This conversation made me think about the following scripture:

Fix these words of mine in your hearts and minds; tie them as symbols on your hands and bind them on your foreheads. Teach them to your children, talking about them when you sit at home and when you walk along the road, when you lie down and when you get up. Write them on the doorframes of your houses and on your gates, so that your days and the days of your children may be many in the land the Lord swore to give your ancestors, as many as the days that the heavens are above the earth.

Deuteronomy 11:18-21

In this passage, Moses is speaking to his people before they enter the Promised Land. It is interesting that today, some orthodox Jews attach small leather boxes (called Tefilin) containing portions of scripture to their arms and forehead at morning prayer times. There is something compelling about this as a reminder of the importance of scripture in their faith. It makes me wonder, how I am "fixing" God's words in my heart and mind? How am I meditating, displaying and passing on His truths?

"May the God of hope fill you with all joy and peace as you trust in him, so that you may overflow with hope by the power of the Holy Spirit."

Romans 15:13

This is one of the scriptures God has directed me to time and time again as I work through changes brought on by my health. I have needed its reminder of hope! I have written

it down in my journal and on note cards around my house. I have meditated on it and asked the Lord what He is teaching me. I've shared it with friends and family as we talk about what God is doing in our lives. I've tried to memorize it and fix the words in my heart and mind as a reminder of the hope that God wants to fill me with. I want this overflowing of hope only found in the power of the Holy Spirit.

What scriptures has God been using in your life lately? Is there a scripture you'd like to spend more time meditating on? Let the Spirit prompt you with a verse or use Romans 15:13 if it impacted you today. Why not write it out on a note card or display it somewhere you will encounter God's living Word throughout your day? Or like my mom, try committing it to memory so that you fix the words in your heart and mind.

And then, let's pass it on!

Put On

It is cold outside today with temperatures well below freezing and a bitter windchill. I try to go for a walk every day and on days like this I know I'll need to think about what I put on before heading out the door. I slide on some snow pants and a heavy coat, wrap a warm scarf around my neck, and pull on a toque and some boots. I'm ready to go! It takes some effort but I am thankful for every piece of clothing when the wind whips around the corner. Today, as I walked, I started thinking about this scripture:

> **Therefore, as God's chosen people, holy and dearly loved, clothe yourselves with compassion, kindness, humility, gentleness and patience. Bear with each other and forgive one another.**
>
> **If any of you has a grievance against someone. Forgive as the Lord forgave you. And over all these virtues put on love, which binds them all together in perfect unity.**
>
> Colossians 3:12-14

What am I clothing myself with each day? Am I asking the Holy Spirit to help me "put on" compassion, kindness, humility, gentleness and patience? Are these virtues evident in my life? When I encounter a situation in my day that feels like a bitter wind whipping around the corner, have I put on forgiveness and humility so I am prepared to respond as God's chosen, holy and dearly loved child? Have I taken the time to put on love above everything?

This is especially important on a day when I'm not feeling well. On those days it can be more challenging to be patient and loving. I want to be known as someone who displays these virtues so people see love as my brightest piece of clothing – not my illness. How about you?

Here's an idea. As you get dressed in the morning ask God to prompt a conscious putting on of each virtue. It may sound silly but as you put on your shirt think about putting on compassion or kindness. As you put on your socks ask the Spirit to fill you with gentleness and patience, and so on. When you put on your coat and head out the door may it bring to mind love – which binds all of the other virtues together.

Take some time to write down each of the virtues mentioned in Colossians 3:12-14. Look up the verses in several translations, or use a thesaurus or dictionary, and see if a different word stands out to you. As you write, talk with God about each. Ask the Spirit to bring to mind an area that may be a struggle and ask for His help. Thank God for the times you have been able to reflect Him through one or more of these traits.

Let's get dressed, my friend!

Raindrops

I love to serve and be available for God. But over the past few years, there have been some changes. At some points, I've had to say no to almost all of the ministry I was previously involved in. Wow – this hurts and frustrates me. What I am now able to offer seems like just a tiny drop of rain.

But God reminds me of how He thinks about "small" things throughout Scripture. God uses small things to make a big impact. Think about the tiny mustard seed (Matthew 13:32), the meagre five loaves and two fish (John 6:9), the poor widow's mite (Luke 21:1-4), and Moses' simple staff (Exodus 4:2).

I believe that what we do for God as a tiny raindrop can be to Him like a crashing waterfall.

As I reflect on my day, my week, my month I ask God to bring to mind some of my "raindrops". He reminds me about the quick phone call to someone, lending an ear to a colleague from work, the card that was sent to share in someone's sorrow, and that video chat with my niece. I feel like He says, "Kara, you see these as small and insignificant raindrops, but I see them as a mighty waterfall of my love." What a shift in perspective!

I still want to look for ways I can be involved in ministry and service, and be available as my body allows, but I want to be sure to see the small acts of service the way He does. They are mighty and powerful representations of His love in this world.

I encourage you today to reflect on your day, week, or month and ask God to bring to mind your "raindrops" for Him. Ask Him to help you see these as a thundering waterfall.

On the facing page take some time to write some of these down (you could even draw droplets around them). Why not come back to this page every now and then and add to it. Allow God to show you that He is using your life. Your service may look different than it used to, but God can turn something small into something mighty.

God can turn something small
into something *mighty.*

Disappointment

I go from hope to disappointment so often.

> Hope because I have a firm diagnosis – but disappointment that it's not going away.
>
> Hope that a new medication will help – but it doesn't.
>
> Hope that there are other medications to try – but then there are immediate side effects.
>
> Hope that I'll be able to go to an activity – but my body is too fatigued.

How about you? Can you think of situations that have moved you from hope to disappointment because of your health?

This constant cycle from hope to disappointment is hard. We know it's normal to feel this way, but we also know we can't linger in disappointment. We know God promises to give us a hope that lasts beyond our circumstances. And we know we need to be able to circle back to a place of hope. The sooner the better. But how?

Two scriptures come to mind. Please don't let their familiarity allow you to miss the fresh word that God may want you to hear in them today.

Now faith is confidence in what we hope for and assurance about what we do not see.
Hebrews 11:1

Therefore we do not lose heart. Though outwardly we are wasting away, yet inwardly we are being renewed day by day. For our light and momentary troubles are achieving for us an eternal glory that far outweighs them all. So we fix our eyes not on what is seen, but on what is unseen, since what is seen is temporary, but what is unseen is eternal.
2 Corinthians 4:16-18

Faith is about being sure of what I hope for even though I can't see it. What do I ultimately hope for? Eternity with God.

These troubles are just for a moment! Even though my body is "wasting away" and disappoints me regularly, I can fix my eyes on the hope of heaven, what is unseen. It

outweighs all the disappointments. Fixing my eyes requires action from me. When I drop my gaze and focus on what is temporary, I can lose my hope and linger in the disappointment.

Of course, disappointments will continue to come (usually right on the heels of hope), but God allows us to catch sight of the eternal again and again. Here is where we find hope!

Take some time to write out or paraphrase 2 Corinthians 4:16-18 today. You can personalize it by replacing "we" with "I." As you write, let God remind you of the truths contained in these verses.

Thank you for the hope of heaven, Father!

Monkey Bars

When was the last time you watched a child swinging on the monkey bars? It's fun to see them learning to move from one rung to the next. To hear their excitement as they yell, "Watch me! Watch me!" But getting from rung to rung doesn't usually happen the first time they try it. It takes a lot of perseverance, many trials, falls, a few tears, and a willingness to reach up to the bars again. On playground supervision, sometimes I've been asked to be a spotter, holding on to their legs to bear some of the weight as they gain confidence to swing their arms forward.

Philippians 3:12-14 says,

> Not that I have already obtained all this, or have already been made perfect, but I press on to take hold of that for which Christ Jesus took hold of me. Brothers and sisters, I do not consider myself yet to have taken hold of it. But one thing I do: Forgetting what is behind and straining toward what is ahead, I press on toward the goal to win the prize for which God has called me heavenward in Christ Jesus.

It seems this verse has been everywhere I turn these days. I have been reflecting on it in light of my current circumstances. I want to let go of what lies behind (the rung I'm on), and press on, or strain toward what lies ahead (the next rung), but I am having trouble doing so. This can be true in many areas of life – ministry involvement, careers, relationships… Is it time to let go and move on to the next rung?

Here is something God has been impressing on my heart.

He is my spotter.

In fact, my arms have been growing very tired hanging from the rung I am on, and sometimes I feel I can't hold on anymore. But God says, "I've got you, Kara." My arms ease from the full weight as He holds me. He is with me in this place of waiting to move on. He's not frustrated with me that I haven't swung ahead yet. He knows I may have to gain confidence here and He promises to stay with me while I wait – with expectant hope that He holds the plans for the future. I don't have to do it alone. He is there and when the time comes He will cheer me on as I swing confidently to the next rung.

Is He calling you to swing forward too? Or is He perhaps saying, "I'll wait here with you?" Could He even be saying, "Stay a while longer on the first rung and deal with something here?"

Would you spend some time talking with Him about this today? Reread the passage from Philippians. Journal some of your thoughts. Picture yourself on the monkey bars of life. Ask Him to hold you, propel you forward, move you back…whatever it is that He speaks to you about. It's not about being perfect but your willingness to press on.

Swing on, my friend.

Psalm 121

I remember always sitting in the same spot on the pink couch when I visited my Great Aunt Susie's house. There was so much to look at – my Aunt Susie was a collector of many things – books, hats, tiny trinkets, and more books. From where I sat I could also see a picture. It was a large framed painting of mountains. What was most interesting to me was the ragged slip of paper taped to the corner. On it were the words, "I lift my eyes up to the mountains – where does my help come from?" As a little girl, I puzzled over these words. What did they mean? Did my help come from the mountains? Over the years I have come to understand its meaning and why my Aunt Susie had this reminder taped to the picture on her wall.

Psalm 121

A song of ascents.

I lift up my eyes to the mountains –
where does my help come from?
My help comes from the Lord,
the Maker of heaven and earth.
He will not let your foot slip –
he who watches over you will not slumber;
indeed, he who watches over Israel
will neither slumber nor sleep.
The Lord watches over you –
the Lord is your shade at your right hand;
the sun will not harm you by day,
nor the moon by night.
The Lord will keep you from all harm –
he will watch over your life;
the Lord will watch over your coming and going
both now and forevermore.

When was the last time you read this Psalm? I have grown to love it and often need its reminder to look up – higher than the mountains – look up to the One who is truly my help. Isn't it amazing that the God who made heaven and earth wants to help each of us? He says He won't fall asleep, He will watch night and day and ensure our care. He will watch over our comings and our goings now and forevermore. He is the Lord. Our chronic illnesses may be invisible to others but we are seen by God.

Today, why not rewrite this Psalm below. Personalize it if you want, instead of "you" write "me". Read it aloud. Say it as a prayer. Let the Lord of all remind you of His boundless love and care for you. We don't have to take on the day alone – the maker of heaven and earth wants to watch over us as we go.

Look UP, my friend!

Rearview Mirror

I was in a car accident – a rear-ender. We had stopped to let a pedestrian cross the street but the person behind us was distracted and drove right into us. As you can imagine, there were some unfortunate consequences from this. Beyond the whiplash and car repairs, something I hadn't expected began to happen when I was driving. I found myself constantly looking in the rearview mirror. I needed to see what the driver behind me was doing. Were they too close? Were they on their phone? I was so concerned with what was going on behind me that I wasn't paying enough attention to what was happening right in front of me. I had to consciously turn my attention forward, and only glance in the rearview mirror occasionally, to drive safely.

A wise friend once said this exact thing to me about my life. "It's pretty hard to drive forward when you're constantly looking in the rearview mirror." Scripture echoes, "Let your eyes look directly forward, and your gaze be straight before you. Ponder the path of your feet; then all your ways will be sure." Proverbs 4:25-26 (ESV)

These days, I have found myself lingering in the rearview mirror of life. Thinking about the way things were before. Travels, ministry, how much energy I had, being able to say yes to many opportunities. Unfortunately, this can cause me to dwell on what is challenging to do now, rather than seeing the road ahead and asking God what He has for me these days. I'm thankful for what was, but I want to look forward with expectant hope and thankfulness for what will be.

God isn't finished with my journey yet – or else I wouldn't be here. He wants to use my life for His purposes but I have to look forward and ask Him to help me ponder the path. He's already shown me some wonderful things along this new leg of my journey. Different ways that He wants to use my life. Ways that He is shaping me into His image even through illness.

Do your eyes want to linger in the rearview mirror? Do you sometimes feel like your best days lay behind you? God wants us to look ahead to what He still has for each of us. Glimpses in the rearview mirror are necessary but we have to set our gaze straight before us to capture all that He still has for us on our journeys.

Take time to write down some of the things you might be lingering on in your rearview mirror. Then ask the Spirit to show you some of the amazing things He is doing in your life today, and for a glimpse of what He may have for you down the road.

Let's look forward with expectant hope!

It's pretty hard to drive forward *when you're constantly looking in the rearview mirror.*

Comparison

In the introduction to this book, I mentioned that I love to search for sea glass. Walking along the beach with the waves tickling at my toes is always a special time for me. Especially coming from land locked Alberta. But I have respect for those gentle waves. I know they can quickly become powerful. Several times in my life I've been surprised by waves – literally being picked up and swirled around – not knowing which way was up. Thankful when I regained my footing.

The Bible talks about being tossed back and forth by waves (Ephesians 4:14; James 1:6). This can happen in many areas of life but today I'm thinking about comparison. We all struggle with comparing ourselves to others throughout our lives... Am I as...?, I wish I had...If only..., etc. When we compare ourselves to others, we become dissatisfied with the plan God has for us – much like being tossed about in the waves.

Over the past few years, I've found I can struggle with comparison when it comes to my illness. For some time I didn't even realize I was comparing, and my pride was involved. Let me explain.

When someone tells me they have a friend with the same illness and they are doing just fine, I wonder why I'm not. When I see someone with a chronic illness working full time, I wonder what's wrong with me. When the medication that works for so many people doesn't work for me, I compare. Every time I compare my journey to someone else's, I get picked up by the waves and can't catch my footing.

God has been dealing with me on this. He wants me to remember that this is the journey He has placed me on and it can't be compared to anyone else's. He wants me to look to Him for my value. And more than anything, to remember that weighing how others are doing with their illness makes me forget the ways that He has blessed me.

On the facing page, take some time with God on this topic. Ask the Holy Spirit to point out areas in your life where you might be comparing and not even realizing it. Ask Him to prompt you about any pride, or if you might be valuing how others see you over how God sees you. Let God remind you of the unique ways He is giving you exactly what you need for your journey.

May we stand solid in our footing not tossed by waves but sure of God's plan.

When we compare ourselves to others, we become dissatisfied with the plan God has for us – much like being tossed about in the waves.

Traffic Circles

Traffic circles – I hate them. I will drive out of my way to avoid them. I find them confusing and hard to navigate. This was especially true in England where you are trying to do everything on the 'wrong' side of the road and from the 'wrong' side of the car too! I remember my friend and I ending up in huge, multi-lane traffic circles as we drove throughout the country. We found ourselves literally driving around and around the circles unsure of how to get out – it was easier to just stay put.

Forgive me for talking about our thought lives again but I feel that God has been impressing upon me that this is a real area of concern for those of us with chronic illnesses. You see, Satan wants to get a foothold here (Ephesians 4:27). He wants us to drive around and around the same circles of thoughts that are not beneficial to us. He tries to convince us that this is easier than trying to navigate off of them onto the path of life that God offers us.

I don't know what your repetitive thoughts are but I know we all have a circle or two we spin around and around in. The enemy loves it when we linger on one of these, such as feeling like a failure because we can't do what we used to. The path to life can only be found if we take the risk to exit the circle and head out in a different direction. On this new roadway, there is an opportunity to choose joy. I want to navigate my way onto God's path, the pathway forward – to life!

You make known to me the path of life;
in your presence there is fullness of joy;
at your right hand are pleasures forevermore.
Psalm 16:11 ESV

Maybe today you could draw a circle and write some of the repetitive, unhelpful thoughts that you allow to go around in your mind. Ask the Spirit to show you what these are, and then draw an exit onto a new path. On this road, you could write words like life, joy, fullness, pleasure... Ask God what He has for you there. Spend time talking with Him about your desire to leave your circular thoughts behind and catch a glimpse of the beautiful road He has for you, even in the midst of your illness or maybe even because of it.

His path is one of fullness and joy if we choose to take it!

On this new roadway, there is an opportunity to

choose joy.

Acceptance

Several years ago I ruptured my Achilles tendon. You're probably thinking this is a very athletic injury and may be wondering how I injured myself. Get ready for a laugh. I was playing Duck, Duck, Goose with my Grade 3 class on the playground at school. I know, it makes me laugh as I think back on it. But at the time it was quite challenging. Three months of non-weight bearing, casts, and crutches. To top it off we were living in the basement of our new house while my husband was renovating the upstairs. A trying time. But – I knew it would come to an end.

A chronic illness isn't going away. It may ebb and flow, it may be managed, but ultimately it's about learning to live with it. Not the way the enemy would have us live – in bitterness – but in God's strength, coming to a place of fullness.

The thief comes only to steal and kill and destroy; I have come that they may have life, and have it to the full.
John 10:10

To the full.

What is that fullness?

Can it be found in our health challenges?

Absolutely!

We don't actually need our outer circumstances to change. The fullness comes through the change in our inner spirit.

Fullness is knowing my salvation comes from Christ. It's the assurance of my heavenly home – my eternal perspective.

And the God of all grace, who called you to his eternal glory in Christ, after you have suffered a little while, will himself restore you and make you strong, firm and steadfast.
1 Peter 5:10

It's not about my health, what I have, or what this world says is important.

It's all about Him. He is fullness.

Here is my prayer. "God, life looks different these days and though I am frustrated by my body there is so much fullness in You. I anticipate life with You – this is fullness. You have provided more than what I need – this is fullness. You offer me salvation – this is fullness. You have given me others who love me – this is fullness. You care enough to refine me into something beautiful – this is fullness. I get to spend time with You – this is fullness. You use everything in my life, nothing is wasted. You even use this illness – this is fullness. Thank you, Father! Amen."

What is fullness to you? Write it out as a prayer to God. Recognize it! Accept it! Maybe your illness is even an entry point to further fullness with Him.

Tree

But blessed is the one who trusts in the Lord,
whose confidence is in him.

They will be like a tree planted by the water
that sends out its roots by the stream.

It does not fear when heat comes;
its leaves are always green.

It has no worries in a year of drought
and never fails to bear fruit.
Jeremiah 17:7-8

I love the picture these verses paint in my mind. This passage always makes me want to pick up some coloured pens and try to sketch out what is being talked about. I like to draw a tree by a stream, add roots stretching beside the water, and some leaves. Then I might add some fruit. My picture is far from beautiful; I am not an artist, but I don't need to be. I just want to give God some space to talk with me about His Word.

As I draw, the Spirit prompts me to reflect on how I, like a tree planted by the water, am doing these days. Where are my roots? Are they too far from the stream, are they fully nourished, are they drawing in nutrients of hope and love? I like to journal these thoughts around my roots.

As I reread the scripture, maybe out loud, I think about my leaves. Are they budding out, are they dry and brittle, are they lush and green? I journal some of these thoughts around my leaves.

How about fruit? I ask the Lord to help me evaluate this in my life. Will I draw some apples on the tree? Am I able to write about what this fruit is? Is there fruit to celebrate? Or is this a time of fruitlessness? Why might this be?

Questions about where my confidence is coming from emerge. Am I fearful at this time? Are there worries I need to bring openly to the Lord? I continue to journal this around my page. My drawing, along with the journaling, starts to give me a good indicator of my spiritual health. Areas to celebrate and areas that may need addressing. A reflective time with God.

I want to encourage you to try this. You don't have to be an artist – remember it's not about how it looks – it's about giving God some space to talk with you about this scripture. Try drawing a simple picture and reflecting on Jeremiah 17:7-8. Prayerfully journal around your tree. May your time with the Lord be blessed as you press close to Him and put your confidence in Him.

Let's stretch our roots beside His nourishing stream today.

Call to Mind

I just got home from an appointment with my specialist. After two years of trying different medications, he told me the last one is doing more good than I realized to prevent further damage in my body from my rheumatoid arthritis. I know this is a good thing but I'm still frustrated. I was hoping we would find something that would take care of more of the symptoms, with fewer side effects.

I'm going to have to accept that this is as good as it gets, for now. Please don't misunderstand, I'm grateful for these medications. But I had hoped we might find "just the thing" to make everything feel wonderful – you know, like in the pharmaceutical commercials!

I'm learning to accept. I will try to pace myself according to how I feel on a given day. Learning to say no when I need to and not feel so guilty. I'm getting better at this.

And I'm also getting much better at letting the Lord be my portion and being thankful that His mercies are new **every** morning. I'm so thankful that each day is a fresh start. These last few years have taught me more than ever to put my hope in Him and that He is good when I seek Him.

Take time with these words from Lamentations 3:21-26.

Yet this I call to mind
  and therefore I have hope:
Because of the Lord's great love
  we are not consumed,
  for his compassions never
  fail.
They are new every morning;
  great is your faithfulness.
I say to myself,
  "The Lord is my portion;
  therefore I will wait for him."
The Lord is good to those whose
  hope is in him,
  to the one who seeks him;
it is good to wait quietly
  for the salvation of the Lord.

I need these verses every day! They offer so much hope. I want to call to mind His steadfastness, mercy, faithfulness, goodness, and salvation. How could I ask for more than His compassion and mercy to face each day?

Would you join me in making this verse part of your morning? Write it out and hang it on your bathroom mirror – that's where my copy is. Recite it aloud as you prepare yourself for the day that lies ahead. Wait on Him to be your portion.

Call His words of hope to mind each morning.

But there's one other thing I
remember,
and remembering, I keep a
grip on hope:
God's loyal love couldn't have
run out,
his merciful love couldn't have
dried up.
They're created new every
morning.
How great your faithfulness!
I'm sticking with God (I say it
over and over).
He's all I've got left.
God proves to be good to the
man who passionately
waits,
to the woman who diligently
seeks.
It's a good thing to quietly
hope, quietly hope for help
from God.

Lamentations 3:21-26 (MSG)

Grandma

My grandma lived to be 99 years old! I'm thankful that I had the blessing of knowing her for so long. She was a very special woman and her faith was an example to me in both its simplicity and its depth. I remember her sharing stories of her life with me. She would often say, "I can see how God's hand was guiding me, just so."

We see that looking back is important throughout Scripture. God gave His people traditions and special occasions, such as Passover, for them to look back. He asked them to stop and be reminded of His faithfulness to Israel. (Psalm 78 is a wonderful example of this.)

How often do we stop and think about how God has been faithful in our lives? I love Psalm 66:5, "Come and see what God has done, his awesome deeds for mankind!"

I want to be ready to share the awesome things God has done for me but to do this, I need to take time to recount them. Looking back on His faithfulness gives me the strength to move forward in confidence with Him, especially in difficult times.

Let's take some time to be reminded of "what the Lord has done" in our lives.

On the facing page you will see a line – turn the page sideways and use this as a timeline of God's faithfulness in your life. Sit with Him and ask Him to remind you of times in your life when He watched over you in a special way; times when you may not have even known of His faithfulness until years later. As it was for my Grandma, it may be that in looking back, you can see "His hand guiding just so."

Think of people He brought into (or out of) your life, provisions He has made in your job, family, health, finances, or safety. What about circumstances that were hard at the time but looking back you can see how they refined you? Or can you recall something that seemed small at the time that was actually life-changing? Plot these out on the timeline in a general order – don't worry if it's exact. Stop to be encouraged and thankful each time you write something down.

I don't know about you, but I needed this today. The encouragement and strength I find in seeing His presence and faithfulness over my life gives me courage and trust for the next days. How about you? Hebrews 10:23 says, "Let us hold unswervingly to the hope we profess, for he who promised is faithful."

Thank you, Father. May we hold on to hope because You are faithful and have shown it time and again!

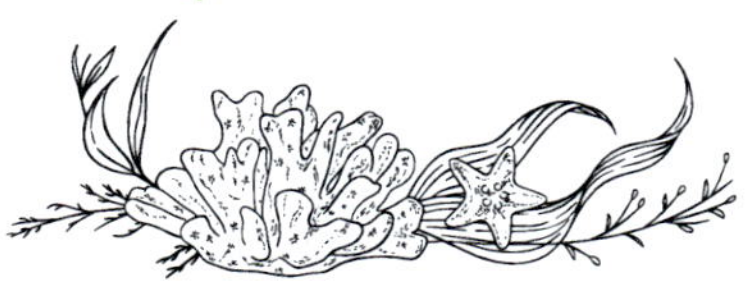

Thy Word

I love going on walking tours when traveling to new places. A few years ago I went on a night tour. We were each given a lantern to carry as we followed the guide. At first, I thought the lanterns simply provided a fun mood but I soon realized that I really appreciated having the light to guide me as we wandered through unfamiliar territory. Having the light in front of me allowed me to see if there was a puddle of water, a rise or fall in the ground, or something that could trip me.

Your word is a lamp to my feet and a light to my path.
Psalm 119:105 (ESV)

I've heard several people talk about this scripture and they often explain how lamps in Bible times were small, oval-shaped bowls, made of clay. They were filled with olive oil and a wick. The lamp would give off a faint light brightening only a small area. If you were walking on a dark night you would probably only be able to see the next step in front of you.

Picturing this deepens my understanding of this scripture and what it means for me today. O, how He wants to guide me on the path I'm on. His Word is a lamp to my feet and a light to my path as I take the next step.

He will guide me.
He is guiding me.
But one step at a time.

And because I know His character, I know that I can trust Him fully for the next step, even if I wish I could see further down the path.

Can you relate? Is there a situation where you wish you knew not just the next step but many down the road? Can you see that God is asking you to trust Him with just that next step? Once we take it we can trust Him for the next and the next. He gives light enough to see each one. What a blessing to be able to give the full journey over to the Lord.

Take some time to pray or journal about your life. Think about how you may need to trust God to give you light for the next step. Ask Him to help you trust that He knows the full pathway. Picture yourself holding up the lamp with just enough light for the next step. You could draw a lamp if you wish. Thank Him for the journey you've already taken with Him and that you can trust Him fully for every step to come.

Thank you, Father, for guiding us one step at a time.

I know I can trust Him fully for the *next step*,
even if I wish I could see further down the path.

Gracious Words

When I was nine, my ten-year-old brother Kent passed away after a three year battle with a brain tumour. Losing my brother at such a young age has shaped me in many ways. I learned that life could be really sad and confusing, but through this I learned about a God who was always there. Kent was such a great brother to me – he would even let me into his forts! But with his illness came times when he didn't feel well enough to play or even say kind words to me. This was hard, even though I knew he was so sick. My brother made me a card in his last months that I still have to this day. In it he wrote these words, "Dear Kara, I'm sorry you've had to be alone and even though I don't show it I want you to know it. I love you." O, how these words, even today, bring a tear to my eye. They are sweet and healing to my soul. Proverbs 16:24 says,

> Gracious words are a honeycomb,
> sweet to the soul and healing to the bones.

Regrettably, the people closest to me often get my worst when I'm not feeling well. I know I can trust them with how I'm really feeling but I too often show them my emotions unchecked. They sometimes get what's left of me but still stick beside me. I'm so thankful for that. My husband is patient to listen to my concerns, willing to do more around the house, and accepts a tired wife. My best friend listens to me, takes me as I am, and has patience with my pain. Most importantly they both pray for me and point me to God.

I can't change the pain, fatigue, and the need to share how I'm feeling. But I can watch that my words are gracious. As it says in Proverbs, I want my words to be like honey, sweet and healing. O, how I want to be intentional about this with the people who stand beside me with such consistency.

Who are your people – the ones who see you at your worst – the ones you can be real with? Are they a spouse, a friend, a family member, or a colleague? Do you feel you could be more intentional about offering them gracious words, sweet to the soul?

Here's what I'm going to do, just like my brother did for me – I'm going to write them a note. And then I'm going to ask the Spirit to prompt and fill me with gracious words – especially on those challenging days.

Will you join me? Find a note card or a simple piece of paper to write on. Recognize what they do for you and express your gratitude for the gift of their relationship in your life.

I bet your words are dripping with honey!

We are all rough and
broken but God uses events,
people, and circumstances in our
lives to wear away the
sharp edges; to soften and shape
us into who He knows
we can be.

Good Work

I thank my God every time I remember you. In all my prayers for all of you, I always pray with joy because of your partnership in the gospel from the first day until now, being confident of this, that he who began a good work in you will carry it on to completion until the day of Christ Jesus.
Philippians 1:3-6

I'm a finisher. If I start something I like to finish it, but I don't always have a lot of patience. I just want to get it done. On the other hand, God is a master finisher who does His work with the utmost patience. We're told in these verses that He started a good work in us and that He is going to complete it. I've often heard this scripture quoted without the last phrase, "until the day of Christ Jesus". God promises His work in us will be complete when Christ returns. Until then, our lives will be God's work in progress.

When we began this devotional journey I talked about sea glass being my reminder of the work God is doing, has done, and is yet to do in my life. His work refining me into a reflection of Him.

I know in my journey there will be many new and repeated refining moments to come as God continues to smooth the rough edges. Having a chronic illness isn't easy but God is faithful to carry on the good work He began in me when I press into Him. I'm so thankful for the way God has met me and for the deepened relationship I have found with Him. I have discovered more and more about who He is and who I am because of this illness.

I so hope that you have found beauty in the refinement as you have journeyed through these devotions. How I pray that you have been pressed into His arms of love and though the refining may be painful, you see the good work He is doing in you.

Today I encourage you to glance back through these devotions and have a conversation with God about what He has done in your life. On the facing page, you could write a prayer of thanks for the good work He is doing in the midst of your health challenges. Thankful that He is walking this path with you – every step – to completion until Christ's return. Thank Him for this hope.

I have loved journeying with you – I just know if I met you it would be like spotting a beautiful piece of sea glass on the beach.

Kara

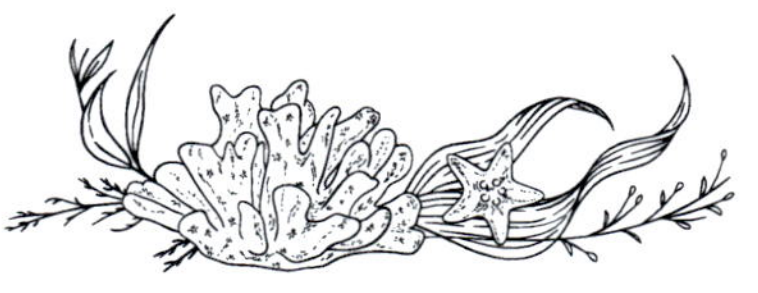

There has never been the slightest doubt in my mind that the God who started this great work in you would keep at it and bring it to a

flourishing finish

on the very day Christ Jesus appears.

Philippians 1:6 (MSG)

Manufactured by Amazon.ca
Bolton, ON

20532122R00040